Growing Up
in Wartime Britain
1939-1945

Published by Alderley Publishing
England

Copyright © 2020 Derek Torrington
All rights reserved

Derek Torrington has asserted his right
under the Copyright, Designs and Patents Act 1988
to be identified as the author of this work

ISBN 978-1-84396-588-6

Also available as a Kindle ebook
ISBN 978-1-84396-589-3

A catalogue record for this book
is available from the British Library and the
American Library of Congress
No part of this book may be copied
or reproduced in any form without the prior
consent of the publisher

Typesetting and pre-press production
eBook Versions
27 Old Gloucester Street
London WC1N 3AX
www.ebookversions.com

Growing Up in Wartime Britain 1939-1945

Derek Torrington
(then aged 8-15)

Alderley Publishing

Contents

1
Preface

3
Chapter One
We "go to the aid of Poland"
and a German bomber flies by

7
Chapter Two
Evacuation, but home again after two days

10
Chapter Three
The Blitz and the beginning of the Churchill effect

14
Chapter Four
Dunkirk and the Battle of Britain

17
Chapter Five
We move to Manchester and life changes greatly

21
Chapter Six
The war turns east and
Soviet Russia becomes an ally

28
Chapter 7
Pearl Harbor and the Americans join in

33
Chapter 8
El Alamein and there is a further shift

38
Chapter 9
We prepare to take the war back into Europe

42
Chapter 10
D-Day and German forces move back to defeat

49
Chapter 11
Victory in Europe and huge celebrations

48
Chapter 12
The post-war world and
ex-servicemen become teachers

53
Chapter 13
It's not over yet

56
Chapter 14
The aftermath

61
Chapter 15
How some things have changed

67
Chapter 16
My last word

Preface

I was eight when Britain declared against Germany.. Now I am 88 and an emeritus professor at the University of Manchester (emeritus means that they don't pay you any longer but let you keep the title for life, as long as you don't do anything to bring the university into disrepute).

This book is not a proper history of the second world war but just a personal account of life growing up in this extraordinary period of human history, although a general intermittent account of the way the war developed is included to give a framework. There is no personal heroism and no analysis, simply narrative and anecdotes, some of which are included in their individual stories. I have culled these from friends and acquaintances.

Their stories include remarkable information. Agnes's story for instance how a draper and a farmer's wife eased the restrictions of rationing by exchanging surplus eggs from the farm for extra tea from the draper's shop and Carolyn tells how her uncle Cecil waited to be rescued at Dunkirk while standing waist-deep in the sea wearing only his underpants.

These memoirs were stimulated by two events. Our elder

daughter has a very good friend, Joanne, who was asking me about life in the war; after chatting to her about odd recollections, she said, "You ought to write a book about it". The second event was that I recently received a letter from the RAF Benevolent Fund, as I was a National Service "veteran", asking how I was and did I need any help. I replied to say that I did not need any help and telling them a little about my service, To which they replied saying "What a story." So here goes.

I write entirely from memory, although I have verified facts available from public record, Google and Wikipedia. My main source of information about the war itself is Antony Beevor's magnificent *The Second World War*, published by Weidenfeld and Nicolson in 2012. Don't be discouraged by its nearly 1,000 pages because it is so absorbing that you can start reading it on a wet Sunday afternoon and suddenly realise hours later that you should have emptied the dishwasher. At my age memory is at best erratic, so there are gaps in this record, but there is no deliberate embroidery to make it a better story.

Chapter One

*We go "to the aid of Poland"
and a German bomber flies past*

In a way, we started it, as British Prime minister Neville Chamberlain took the step of declaring war on Germany "to the aid of Poland". Successive attempts at appeasing Adolf Hitler's claims for Lebensraum, or living space. Sudetentland, a part of northern Germany, had been ceded to Czeckoslavakia after the first World War and given back to Germany in 1938 in an early attempt at appeasement, but Czechoslavakia itself was overrun in 1939, using the novel method of defenestration, or throwing people out of windows. The people thrown out were Czech politicians refusing to accept occupation. Austria was also occupied, but Chamberlain made a belated last stand by committing to military action in aid of Poland if there was any aggressive German move, and demanding assurance from Berlin by a specific date.

Germany invaded Poland on 1st September. Although it was eighty years ago and I was only eight, I remember it clearly. My mother, my older brother and I were in a holiday bungalow in Lancing, Sussex, which we had acquired in 1938; my father was at home in London It was Sunday, 3rd September. During the morning a rather officious Air Raid Warden called to tell us that our blackout protection had not been adequate the previous evening. My mother didn't like his manner and said. "We haven't declared war yet. To which he replied, "Hitler went into Poland on Friday and Chamberlain is on the wireless at 11 this morning." We listened to the broadcast as Neville Chamberlain solemnly explained that Berlin had not produced the requisite assurances, so Britain and France now consider themselves at War with Germany.

Our bungalow was about half a mile from the beach. Standing in the garden and looking west you could see the imposing building of Lancing College Chapel. That afternoon I was messing about in the front garden when there was the sound of an aircraft, flying low and slow. I called my mother and brother to watch as it gradually appeared, passed and soon turned to go back seaward.

My father arrived, having heard the news on the radio, and soon took us back to London. The aircraft was identified by my brother Keith as a Dornier fliegende bleistift or flying pencil as it had a large bubble at the front for the pilot and navigator, a long cylindrical fuselage and a smaller bubble at the back for a rear gunner, who waved condescendingly as they flew into the distance. I therefore claim to be one of a very small number of people still alive who saw an enemy aircraft over England on the day World War 2 began. You may scoff and regard that story as ridiculous; how could it have reached Lancing from the nearest German base in Essen? My mother and elder brother are no longer with us to offer corroboration, but I saw it, I believe it, so there.

Home was in Hornsey north London. where my father was General Secretary of the Hornsey Y.M.CA, to provide accommodation and recreation for young men who had moved out of the family home to work in the nearby city. The Hornsey building was new and we lived next door at 52, Elmfield Avenue. I attended Rokesley Primary School on the other side of the road and older brother Keith was at the Stationers' Company School half a mile away.

I never understood how my father was able to afford a seaside bungalow as it was a rare luxury in those days. I know it suffered war damage of some sort and my father received compensation.

Notes

Air Raid Wardens were volunteers with the job of patrolling the streets from dusk to ensure that black-out protections against air raids were being observed. No lights should be seen, street lighting was virtually eliminated and motor vehicles had masked headlights. If enemy aircraft were actually observed approaching an area, a siren would be sounded and everyone was to seek shelter. When official observers decided the danger had passed a different type of sound would signal "all clear" but the black-out remained.

Wireless was the conventional term for a radio set in the house, contained in a piece of furniture designed for the purpose. It had to be plugged into the electric circuitry of the house. Portable radios did not exist, neither did television as a means of information and entertainment. It first became widely available in 1953, when we watched Queen Elizabeth II being crowned on our small television set together with some of our neighbours.

The YMCA features a great deal in this book, so more information at this point is appropriate, especially as the term was widely used in popular music recently with a slightly different emphasis. The YMCA was a number of charitable bodies established in the Victorian period. YMCA is a world-wide body and Keith, after studying history at Cambridge, collaborated with an American academic in writing a history of the first hundred years of the YMCA.

Chapter Two

Evacuation, but only for two days

Returning from Lancing in time to go back to school, both Keith and I received some disconcerting news: we were to be evacuated later in the week. Some weeks earlier the government had anticipated that German bombers would carry out extensive bombing raids across the south east of England in a process of undermining British morale. Consequently a programme was begun to evacuate children and vulnerable adults from towns and cities to safer places in the countryside. It was obviously a voluntary procedure, but many children were moved. However the bombing had not then happened, so most of the children returned.

Now the bombing was to happen after all and a second wave of evacuation was being organised. Our parents decided that Keith and I were to be included in the evacuation of boys at his school with any siblings, to be billeted together, staying with a family. Teachers and their families were to accompany us, travelling by train to the town of Wisbech in East Anglia, where we would share the facilities of the local secondary school on a two shift basis They would be having lessons from early morning until lunchtime and we would take their places from lunch time until late afternoon.

The first blow was that we were not to live together after all. Keith was to be in a large house, alone with a widow, who was not willing to have more than one evacuee. A teacher took him off to his new billet, while his wife looked after me by giving me toast and marmalade on a pleasantly warm day. Then the teacher returned, had a quick cup of tea, and took me off to my billet. It was with a childless couple of, I suppose, thirty. He was a painter and decorator; his wife was loud and fat. They lived in a terraced house with a single toilet, outside. As a special treat we had fish and chips for supper and I went to sleep in a large bed, with a chamber pot underneath. I was not happy.

The following day was Saturday and Keith came to collect me after I had had a pretty good breakfast, and we walked round Wisbech, going to the cinema to see a William film.

Sunday my parents arrived to see how I was getting on (remember, no mobile 'phone). There was no 'phone at all in my billet, so no contact beforehand). I Remember little of the meeting, but realised that my mother took a strong dislike to the wife and to the toilet arrangement. We moved on to pick up Keith and found a cafe for lunch. The decision was made that fourteen year old Keith should remain as his accommodation was reasonable and he needed to wait and take his School Certificate exams after coming home for Christmas, while I would return immediately with my parents to Hornsey.

By that time we had two bomb shelters. The Anderson shelter was in the back garden, made of corrugated iron and built like a large dog kennel,1.8 metres tall, 4.5 wide and 2.00 metres long. designed for six people

The Morrison shelter came in March 1941, and was for

internal use, made of sheet steel top and bottom and wire mesh grill for the sides, 1 metre tall, 5.5 metres long and 4.55 metres wide.

The idea for both was the same: when you heard the air raid siren the family clustered inside the shelter, getting to know each other really well. When the "All clear" sounded, you all tumbled out and formed an orderly queue for the toilet or the shower, though that was a rare luxury in those days. Neither shelter could withstand a direct hit but the Anderson could cope with falls of external masonry and the Morrison with internal masonry and flying glass. In some houses it was used as a dining table between air raids.

For whatever reason these shelters were not available to everyone so alternatives were some made by householders.

Arthur's story

I was a child in Liverpool when war broke out and in preference to an Anderson or Morrison shelter my father acquired some railway sleepers which were placed diagonally from floor to ceiling in the lounge of our house as a protection against blast and any falling debris if the house was damaged. I remember the excitement of deconstructing this on a sunny week-end when the war was over and, for me, enjoying a lounge for the first time.

Anther idea was to use the basements of large buildings. The largest use was of the London Underground system and its platforms being used at night by thousands of Londoners, who would go down after the trains had stopped, taking bedding and supplies for the night.

The war was beginning to affect families, as conscription

took effect. On the afternoon that war was declared, Parliament passed legislation that all males between the ages of 18 and 41 had to register for military service. This was later raised to 51. Later the "call up" was extended to unmarried women between 20 and 30, including childless widows. There were exemptions on the grounds of ill health and being employed in an essential occupation, which included farming and engineering as well as the obvious medical professions and others.

Conscientious objectors could be excused military service, if they could convince a tribunal of the genuineness of their objection. They were then required to be employed in, or find employment in, an essential occupation. Those unable to comply were put to work in mining and were nicknamed "Bevin Boys" after Ernest Bevin the Minister of Labour. Many of those in essential occupations did additional work to support the war effort.

Philip's story

My grandfather Jack Peacock was employed by the Oldhams' Battery factory in Denton, East Manchester employed in the essential occupation of manufacturing miners' lamps, but he was keen "to do his bit" extra so he served throughout the war as an auxiliary fireman.

Notes

Evacuation Evacuees went to varied destinations, often to relatives, but mostly in groups, usually no more than ten to fifteen miles away, but some much further; some certainly went to Canada, occasionally remaining after the war was over.

Scott's story

I was at school in South Manchester when my father, who dealt in paint, heard that another local businessman, Charles, was planning to evacuate his family to Canada to stay with relatives until he could re-establish himself there and they would be happy if Scott wanted to come with them. To my surprise my father agreed, and it sounded exciting, so I had to get myself packed and organised to leave on the SS Benares departing in a week's time.

Two days later it was all off as there was no space for me on the ship. A week later it was torpedoed by a German submarine in the North Atlantic and 77 evacuee children died. The evacuation of The Stationers Company School, in which Keith and I were involved, was an example of a whole school including staff and their families being evacuated, another example was Roedean, the elite independent school in Sussex near Brighton, which moved up to the Station Hotel in Keswick in Cumbria, over 350 miles away. "Safe" areas were identified and local authorities ordered to identify appropriate accommodation to receive one or more evacuees.

It was obligatory to accept, which was not always welcome to householders, and in some towns when a trainload of evacuees arrived they were lined up in the public square for prospective welcoming families could pick out the one they wanted, rather like a slave market. In most cases, however, it was successful. I was not the only one with a bad experience. Official estimates put the number of places required at over 5,000, 000, only 3,000,000 places were taken.

Dorothy's story

I was born in Glasgow and was badly affected by the bombing, so that I suffered a form of what would be called post traumatic stress disorder. I had a form of paralysis preventing me from speaking and limiting limb movements. A puzzled consultant in the hospital suggested getting me away from Glasgow, so the whole family of four evacuated itself to a relative in the North and lived for three years in the front room of a small terraced house. Recently I have re-visited the house that we spent three years in that one small room. I could not believe it.

Notes

Billets This was a familiar term applied to military personnel but not to children, and it was normally staying with families on similar terms as fostering.

William (the name of the film Keith and I saw) was William Brown, who was leader of a small gang of boys about my age who got into harmless mischief like embarrassing his elder sister Ethel and irritating much older brother Robert. The books were by an unmarried lady, Richmal Crompton, who wrote 39 books in a series starting in 1922. They were immensely popular. The group of boys called themselves "The Outlaws". Their great hate was a girl named Violet Elizabeth Bott, who got so cross with them that she threatened to…"cry and cry until I am thick.".

Chapter 3

The Blitz and the Churchill effect

Back in Hornsey, it was back to Rokesley primary school for me. I retain little recollection of experience in the school except that there was a pantomime at Christmas and one of the young teachers appeared as a good fairy wearing a diaphanous skirt through which could be discerned a woman's legs, a rare sight!

The school had a barrage balloon in its grounds, together with a set of anti-aircraft guns. Rokesley Primary school, which still exists, at that time separated boys from girls, so I can only speak about boys. We sat in rows of individual desks with an attached bench seat. The desk had a hinged lid with odd books and paraphernalia underneath. On top at the front was a narrow trough for pencils and pens with nibs and a single inkwell for black ink. Fountain pens came when one was older. Biros and rollerball pens were unknown.

A feature of everyday life from this time until after the end of the war was rationing, due to the difficulty of obtaining goods from overseas. First came petrol, then food, including followed by clothing and furniture. Food rationing started by limiting as an example, butter to 57 ounces per person, per week, margarine to 113 ounces and lard to 57 ounces. Bacon, ham, meat, cheese, sugar, tea, milk, preserves and sweets were all limited. The only exemptions were fruit and vegetables, although many were limited by supply and demand; I never saw a banana, orange, grapefruit or other exotica until years after the end of the war. The aim was that everyone had an equal share of what could be produced in Britain to maintain a universal basic nutritional diet. Everyone was issued with a personal ration book of food stamps to exchange with your payment in shops.

Although an inconvenience, the basic allowance produced a better diet than many people had previously followed. The limitations were gradually relaxed at the end of the war, as supply improved. Sweets were the last to be de-rationed.

The next development was the Blitz, which started towards the end of 1940 and continued into 1941. 30,000 people were killed and as many were injured in London alone and huge swathes of the capital were destroyed. King George and Queen Mary regularly visited bombed areas; when a bomb caused some damage at Buckingham Palace, where they were living The Queen reportedly said, "Now we can look the East End in the face".

My personal memories from this period are first collecting shrapnel on the way to school, shrapnel being metal fragments that came from bombs that had exploded, casting bits widely. We boys compared our discoveries with each other in the playground. My second recollection is if going to my desk next to my friend Bannister in the classroom, only to find that had not come to school that day. Later a teacher came in crying to tell the class that a bomb had fallen on his house and all the family had been killed. Later she put a jam far with some flowers on his desk, after collecting all his belongings from it; she was still crying.

What turned out to be a most significant event was on10th of May 1940: Winston Churchill became Prime Minister. Neville Chamberlain was obliged to resign and King George VI sent for Churchill and asked him to form a coalition government involving senior members of the Labour Party. Apart from Churchill, Anthony Eden (Conservative) was Secretary of State for War, Clement Atlee (Labour) was Deputy Prime Minister and Herbert Morrison (Labour) Home Secretary. They faced a dire situation as the Germans swept through France after Holland and Belgium surrendered. Paris would soon follow.

My purpose in this book is not tell the story of WW2, but the story of growing up in it, and part of that story is of hearing, and occasionally seeing, Winston Churchill during that period.I listened to one of his most significant speeches at this point. It was on the radio in our house with my parents. I was still not yet 9 years old, but knew that all our allies had been over-run and we were likely to be invaded. The speech in the House of Commons was quite long, but I remember quite clearly one passage:

"...we shall defend our island, whatever the cost may be, we shall fight on the beaches, we shall fight on the landing grounds, we shall fight in the fields and in the streets, we shall fight in the hills; we shall never surrender."

The passage was delivered with a steadily increasing volume and slight increase in speed until the last four words, and for those the pace and volume dropped and the delivery was almost like a throwaway remark, as if stating the blindingly obvious.

Recently a film was produced called "The Darkest Hour" about this period, with Gary Oldham playing the part of Churchill. Those four words were delivered quite differently, rising to a crescendo with a triumphant shout and eliciting excited waving of order papers by the House of Commons members. It wasn't like that on the 18th June 1940, my ninth birthday!

Agnes's story: My father ran a draper's shop, and unusually he also dealt in tea (a rationed item), which had to be carefully weighed and packaged for each individual customer, one of whom was Mrs Preston, a farmer's wife who kept hens. Every week she delivered 20 eggs to our house, which was much more than the ration, so we kept the surplus by immersing them in Isinglass, a kind of gelatine derived from sturgeon. I always wondered why my father always weighed out the tea for Mrs Preston

As far as possible we had to be self-sufficient in food, just as we were self-sufficient in coal in the days before we worried about its polluting effects. Food is a topic that will recur in this book.

Mary's story

I lived in Jarrow when war broke out and my father was in the merchant Navy. On his rare spells of shore leave he always came home with items of food that he had garnered while away. In particular I remember chocolate and tinned fruit. On one occasion we didn't see him for eighteen months after he was shipwrecked of the west coast of Africa. He still managed to bring home some tins of fruit.

Notes

A barrage ballon was a very large dirigible shaped roughly like an airship that was inflated and allowed to float upwards while linked by cable to a solid base on the ground. The purpose was to discourage or disable Stuka dive bombers. Relatively small,the

Stuka dived straight down towards their target and pulled up from the dive after releasing their bombs. At this point they might be brought down by a barrage balloon cable.

Anti-aircraft guns were ground-based artillery with a long range capability to destroy enemy aircraft.

Blitz/litzkrieg was developed to avoid the horrors of trench warfare in WW1 which resulted in tens of thousands of men literally bogged down on both sides and making no progress. The blitz notion was initiated by the British between the wars as a concept of having a sustained lightning strike to achieve either victory or total ascendency quickly. The Germans used the method in 1940 by heavy bombardment from aircraft directed at London and other British cities, notably Coventry. The destruction was extensive.

Chapter 4

Dunkirk and the Battle of Britain

Now we come to a pivotal moment in the war. France was split in two. The south was in the hands of The Vichy government, stretching from the town of Vichy and down across the south. Set up in 1940, it was run by Marshal Petain, a hero of World 1and Chief Minister Pierre Laval, who hated the British. It was a dictatorship willing to collaborate with the Germans. The British Expeditionary Force was retreating towards the Channel as slowly as possible to allow as many fighting troops to be gathered at Dunkirk as could get there, while slowing the German advance by heavy long range bombardment from the Royal Navy. By the end of May troops were gathering at Dunkirk to evacuate as many as possible, with an Admiralty estimate of being able to save 45,000. Then the deployment began of 600 amateur sailors and their "little ships" such as yachts, cabin cruisers, river vessels and in-shore pleasure craft. They shuttled two and fro between Dunkirk either to collection points on the English coast or to larger Royal Navy ships anchored further out. Many of the troops had been waiting in water up to their armpits.

Carolyn's story

My uncle Cecil, who I never knew as he died when I was very small, was in the army at Dunkirk and was waiting for rescue in the water, wearing only his underpants. At first he had been picked up by one of the smaller "little ships" but this was sunk by an enemy rifle shot, so he abandoned all his kit which was wet through and very heavy, so he was able to swim out to one of the Royal Navy ships. D-Day was still over a year away, but all the Dunkirk veterans were not deployed in those landings as it was thought unwise to risk them on the Normandy beaches.

One item of memorabilia I have from Uncle Cecil is the menu from Christmas 1944 celebratory meal in Brussels, six months after D-Day, in honour of the British liberators. The Menu included included la velute Reine Elizabeth, le dindoneau Roti a la Brioche, Le Carre de Pave Roti, Legumes de Saison, Le Pouding de Noel, Les Mince Pies, Dessert, The, Beer, Cigarettes, Cigars.

On reading Carolyn's story and having seen the full menu, I find it astonishing that the Belgians were able to provide that menu within hours of D-Day.

My father had come home with the news that troops were gathering in Dunkirk, "and the Navy will pick them up in the morning." How wrong he was: the Dunkirk evacuation lasted from 26th May till 4th June. How wrong The Admiralty was with the estimate of rescuing 45,000, 338,000 were collected from Dunkirk, predominantly British, but also a number of Free French. It was well described as "The Miracle of Dunkirk", which boosted morale, but it was still a defeat. The Battle of Britain was soon to follow.

The Battle of Britain was the first battle waged exclusively in the air. With the Battle for France now over and Britain still refusing to surrender despite the Blitz Hitler ordered Goering to bomb all the military airports in southern England as a preliminary to invasion. The German military generals were alarmed, as they had collectively suffered significant losses in both the Battle of France and the fighting in the low countries. In total the Luftwaffe had lost 1, 280 aircraft in the same period that Britain lost 930. Also, after a very late start to re-armament inthe1930s the rate of manufacturing new aircraft had increased markedly.

Additional benefit was air force personnel who had escaped from the German invasion of their land with their aircraft. Their commander was General Sikorski, a veteran of WW1, who reluctantly agreed that their airmen and aircraft being integrated with the RAF, despite differences in culture and language; few of the fliers had more than a few words of English and feared being shot down over England and regarded as German because of their language. Their commitment and skill surpassed that of the British as they were battle-hardened in fighting the Germans in the vain attempt to protect their homeland from occupation in 1939. They were all fearless fighters, although their aircraft were older and slower than the Germans.

The Royal Air Force could deploy 2,350 aircrew, together with 750 other nationalities, including Australians, Canadians, New Zealanders, South Africans, Poles and French. The RAF used hurricanes and Spitfires, of which the Spitfire proved to be the most effective in the close order conflict that characterised the aerial dog fights that took place over the south of England in the summer of 1940from 10th July to 30th June.

The German bombers were Messerschmidts, Dorniers, which you may remember from the very beginning of this book, and Stukas. These were dive bombers that dived from a great height to very near the ground and then pulled up and dropped its bombs before making its escape. they were prone to destruction by anti-aircraft attack when pulling up out of the dive. Initially they attacked airfields to put them out of action, but then moved to civilian targets. The fighting was very hard on pilots and the aircraft.

They had to be ready for action by sunrise and then sat around in their full flying kit until they were called by loud speaker to "scramble" when they ran to their aircraft and climbed into their cockpit to run through routine safety checks and taxiing for takeoff and up, up and away with the objective of locating an enemy aircraft then using your machine gun which was designed to fire between the spinning blades of the single propeller so the pilot got reasonably close to the enemy aircraft and pointed his plane to the other in order to fire a short burst until it was disabled. If the pilot was able to eject from the plane and inflate his parachute, he would not be fired at as he descended, a policy the Poles found difficult to understand.

The battle produced heroes for people to admire. One was Douglas Bader, who qualified as a pilot before the war, but then had a motor accident resulting in both legs being amputated below the knee. With the assistance of prosthetics he returned to flying and enlisted with the R.A.F and scored a number of victories until he was shot down over northern France and imprisoned in a prisoner of war camp at St Omer, having lost one of his prosthetics. The R.A.F then managed a remarkable achievement: first they heard of his predicament, then they located the company that had manufactured the prosthetic and ordered a replacement, which was delivered in days. then they despatched a light aircraft, bearing R.A.F Insignia which flew across the Channel between two nations at war with each other and dropped the prosthetic into the prison yard without a shot being fired from either side. Bader made several escape attempts but was eventually transferred to Colditz castle, where he was eventually liberated by American troops in 1945.

Notes:

Polish allies The difficulty of some Poles being thought of as German was neatly illustrated by two incidents found by Antony Beevor for his history,. one was the Pole with very limited English. He landed in a field and saw a group of men running towards him with pitchforks.He used the only English he knew and said, "fuck off". The cry went up, "It's all right. He's one of ours." before taking him off for refreshment. The other was a man with good English who found he had parachuted into the grounds of an up market tennis club, whose members all seemed quite old. They welcomed him warmly and signed him in as a guest, rooted around to find an old racket, some spare white flannels and offered him a game.

He played with considerable vigour against a series of opponents, who quickly flagged, until the RAF van arrived to take him back where he belonged. Where else in the world would you find a situation in which a group of people would pay such attention to social niceties in welcoming a strange flyer who had just "dropped in" with his parachute,while aerial dog fights were raging above?

Douglas Bader was a considerable personality. much decorated.

he retired as a Group Captain. The story of his life by Paul Brickhill called "Reach for the Sky" was turned into a film.

There were inevitably casualties on both sides In the battle but the German losses were greater; in July and August the RA.F lost 700 aircraft while the Luftwaffe lost over 2,000. At home there were regular reports on the radio about the losses. I remember after one daily report my mother threw up her hands and pronounced, "How can he (Hitler) possibly go on?" The Battle of Britain was begun by Hitler in order to draw the teeth of the RAF to ensure air superiority for the projected invasion. My mother was right and Hitler postponed invading Britain and turned to another enemy. As the Battle of Britain drew to its close Churchill produced two more of his timeless statements, first about the battle that had ended;

"Never in the field of human conflict has so much been owed by so many to so few, and then about the future relations with Russia,"

"I can not forecast to you the action of Russia. It is a riddle wrapped in a mystery inside an enigma."

Chapter Five

We move to Manchester and life changes greatly

Early in 1941 there was a big change as my father was to take over the YMCA in Manchester, and we moved to a very different environment. Hornsey was a suburb of London, Manchester YMCA was in the Centre of Manchester near Central Station, next door to the Free Trade Hall on one side and the Midland Hotel (Where Rolls and Royce had set up their partnership over lunch) on the other. The YMCA and the Midland had been built by the same architect late in the nineteenth century, both extremely solid big Victorian buildings. The YMCA had offices and catering outlets on the ground floor, then a mix of concert halls and meeting rooms followed by a gymnasium and running track above a full size swimming pool at the top. There was a single lift.

Unlike Hornsey, we did not live next door, but in the outer suburb of Brooklands,10 miles away, In quite a large house with cellars and an attic bedroom. I had a bedroom at the back with a view of the playing fields of Sale High School for Boys. I soon discovered a small gate that I could use to get on to the playing field when nobody was about and practice my off breaks, so this was all right for me, but my mother was not sure about the YMCA,

Grace's story

I was taken into the lovely Noton Barclay lounge, in the dim light I could see three old men prostrate on three settees with newspapers over their faces. When I said we had made a terrible mistake Reg..reassured me:"I'm going to change all this; we must turn this place into a great headquarters for the Forces until the end of the war". By the end of July the Noton Barclay Lounge had been transformed and was now our main canteen. Volunteer ladies were recruited and grouped into shifts to cover every 24 hours. It never closed its doors, day or night until some time after the end of the war .It was formally opened by H.R.H The Princes Royal.

My father was very imaginative and determined;. he discovered that there were extensive disused railway properties behind the YMCA building, so he went to see the Forces welfare officer for Western Command, who spoke to the War Office and the railway properties were commandeered for use by the YMCA. It was duly converted into dormitory accommodation for military personnel. Another call went out for ladies to volunteer for the duties of bed making and cleaning. Again there were a lot of volunteers anxious" to do their bit in the war effort".

In Manchester one wing of the main YMCA building was turned into an officers' club with single bedrooms and a lounge, requiring another recruitment of volunteer ladies.

At this point I diverge in order to tell you about British Restaurants. This was an innovation in 1940 by the Minister of Food, Lord Woolton, and lasted until 1947. Their purpose was to provide cheap, basic healthy meals for people who had been bombed out, had used up all their ration coupons or were in some other form of need. At their peak there were over 2,100 throughout the country. In Manchester it was on Oxford street opposite Oxford Road Station. A staple was tripe and onions.

Notes

Grace As you may have guessed, Grace was my mother, a semi retired opera singer, who first met my father when he was secretary of the YMCA in Brighton and she used to sing to groups of soldiers, waiting to go across the Channel to join the fighting in WW1. Henceforth in this book I will refer to my parents as Reg. and Grace, terms I would never dreamed of using in their lifetime, but it saves space! When we arrived in Manchester he was 48 and she was 41. Late in life she produced a short memoir and Grace's story above is an extract from it.

Commandeered This term is virtually unknown these days, but it refers to the power of government to take over premises, with or without compensation for military use.

Chapter Six

The war turns east and Russia becomes an ally

Winning the Battle of Britain was a major step forward, although Britain did not immediately realise this, and bombing continued at night for some time while British bombing of Berlin and major industrial cities developed. Among these was the remarkable dam busters raid, an account of which comes later.

Apparently Hitler had decided that Britain could wait a year in view of the Luftwaffe's humiliation. Instead he invaded Russia. This was a long-term aim to destroy the heart of communism, which he believed the Americans would support. He eventually invaded on22nd June 1941 and initially made good progress with his Panzer divisions of tanks rolling over the east European plain, which the Russians could not match but the mud of Autumn and the freezing cold of a Russian winter slowed their advance dramatically.

The British victory by the Few also had a powerful effect on opinion in the USA.. For some time President Roosevelt had thought of helping the British, but others had disagreed, mainly a group headed by Senator Joe Kennedy, father of John. F, Robert and Edward. The Dunkirk news had impressed the Americans and the Battle of Britain success convinced Roosevelt and he ordered his military commanders to make plans.

Hitler's decision to invade Russia stemmed from his obsession about racial purity and the total superiority of the Aryan race (blond-haired, blue-eyed Germans) and his insane obsession with the need to eliminate untermenschen or lower peoples. mainly Jews but also Russians; and for those two groups there were additional reasons. He declared that Jews were behind most banks and plutarchy in general, while the Russians were Communists, bent on spreading Communism throughout Europe.

By now this truly was a <u>World</u> war. In addition to Britain and her allies engaged with Germany in Europe there was a civil war in Spain,with Germany in support of the Cuadilla, Italy had invaded Albania, Ethiopia and British Somalia. In the Far East Japan had invaded China and would soon take over much of South East Asia. It was all a bit beyond a nine year old to make sense of, but one thing I <u>did</u> grasp was that we were fighting Germany and lots of countries had already joined in on our side; now Russia had been invaded, so they were on our side as well.

There were some communists in Britain, including two MPs and Hewlett Johnson, who was a senior Anglican Cleric, although he never joined the Communist Party. Generally British opinion was anti-communist because of its atheism, and this was certainly the view in the Torrington household and we acknowledged that Mr Churchill had said we would help them technically and economically: they were our ally. So my life just went on as usual as 1940 became 1941, the bombing lessened and I neared 10, collecting conkers rather than shrapnel. We had a family Christmas with Keith home but then to return to Wisbech and soon take School Certificate.

Chapter Seven

Pearl Harbor and the Americans Join in

As the year proceeded into Autumn, Hitler's tank rush of conquest in Russia slowed and then stopped at the gates of Moscow. In December Japan attacked Pearl Harbor in Hawaii, killing over 2.000 American personnel and destroying a significant part of the American pacific naval fleet. Hawaii was a state of the USA, closer to Los Angeles than Los Angeles was to New York, so this was very close to home and American declaration of war against Japan followed on December 11th. A third significant act in this month was that President Roosevelt authorised the beginning of research into the development of a nuclear weapon.

Back home all of these developments seemed far away and bemusing, but there was a lot going on. Keith was now home, having completed an admirable School Certificate. In September he joined History sixth in The Manchester Grammar School (never forget the definite article).

If Reg had undertaken a commercial career instead of the YMCA, ..he would have undoubtedly become a millionaire. he had great drive and presence, this coming from being in the

Coldstream Guards in WW1 until being invalided out with a complaint known in those days as "smokers heart".

In Manchester he developed great skill as a fundraiser, as none of his projects could have been realised without money. The War Office could commandeer a set of buildings, and Grace could produce squads of women volunteers, but bills had to be paid and equipment purchased. Money was raised in various ways. .A typical method at the time was to invite a member of the Royal Family to come and accept purses from people or groups who genuinely wanted to contribute, especially if they could briefly meet royalty, perhaps also being visible in a photograph.

The main method, however, was by eliciting contributions from companies and other businesses. He started with the members of the YMCA board, one of whom was Sir William Mather, Chairman of a large engineering company in the industrial area of Manchester. He and other board members produced generous donations and provided numerous introductions to potential donors, who Reg then visited, always leaving with a donation. He believed that all the donations came with a genuine desire to "do one's bit", although some were enhanced by a wish to give more than a competitor. Two very fruitful introductions were the Lord Mayor of Manchester and the Bishop of Salford.

The Lord Mayor at the time was Jewish and was initially surprised to have a visit from a secretary of the Young Mens' Christian Association and began the conversation by saying," Well I'm only a Jew", which sounds today to be remarkably diffident. Hitler's determination to exterminate the Jewish people produced many donations.

Although the trigger for America to join in had been Pearl Harbor, American troops began to arrive in large numbers at various locations in Britain, predominantly in the south east, as there were two phases of the war in which they would be involved. First was partnering RAF bomber command in raids on Germany. Secondly was preparation to invade France and Italy and move on to Germany. Suddenly there were lots of likeable young Americans, who spoke a strange version of English properly, arriving in places throughout the country.

The first contingents came in January 1942 with numbers increasing to three million in 1944. They had two nicknames; they saw themselves as G.Is. which was short for Government issue; The British saw them as Yanks, a term popularised in WW1, short for Yankee. Their English was not quite right, but they were still very likeable wearing much smarter uniforms that the British as well as being better paid, leading to the envious jingle, "Over sexed, over paid and over here". Their British counterparts in the Army and the RAF had uniforms of serge, while the Americans had a mixture of nylon and fine twill fabric. 70,000 British women left Britain to marry Americans when the war was over, as did 20,000 German women. They were known as GI Brides.

Chapter Eight

El Alamein and there is a further shift

The war took another turn by fighting in north Africa. Why north Africa? It all begins with the Greeks and Romans, who at different times held territory there. That led to the age of colonial expansion and European interest in the 19th century. The British and French squabbled over Egypt, Italy grabbed Libya, France had Algiers, making it a part of France until independence in the 20th century.

Hitler reluctantly agreed with his military commanders that an offensive along north African coast would be a sound move to improve their position in the Mediterranean with its access to the oilfields of the Middle East. They envisaged a quick campaign, but it dragged on as Commonwealth forces arrived to help repel the German advance, but the climax came with the battle of El Alamein on the border between Egypt and Libya. On 23rd October 1942 German and British troops were amassed on opposing sides of the border. as darkness fell a lone Scots piper played his bagpipes at a position at the top of the British troops, walking slowly along the lines, the haunting music floated over to the Germans. At daybreak the British

Eighth army attacked the German lines supported by air strikes from the RAF and US aircraft, recently arrived to join the allied struggle.. The battle continued into November but eventually the Germans withdrew.

This battle was significant in various ways: It gave a boost to morale among the troops and at home. The Battle of Britain had given us our first victory, now we had a land battle victory as well. It was the first time that British and Commonwealth troops had American troops alongside them. We had new heroes so that those who were at El Alamein became known as 'The Desert Rats'. Their commander was General Bernard Law Montgomery, an ascetic, non-smoking teetotaller, he was apparently very well-regarded by his troops, and later became Lord Montgomery of El Alamein.He was also the figurehead of Reg's last big project, still some time in the future.

Allied troops now moved along the north African coast, pushing the Germans back and rescuing communities that had been briefly under German control. .Before this push the Germans were in frisky mood, confidently looking forward to arriving in Cairo and its fleshpots after spending weeks in the desert in the company of flies, cockroaches and overpowering heat. Someone, I don't remember who, said that a telegraph message was sent to 'the ladies of Cairo' saying, liberation is at hand, get out your best dresses and prepare for good times.

I was now eleven, and at school a nativity play was to be staged in which I was to play Joseph. At a boys school there are no girls, so a parent who was also the producer, found two suitable girls, a brunette to be Mary and a blonde to be the Angel Gabriel. After the final performance two boys who lived near me and I started to walk home also, accompanied by

Gabriel. When we reached my house we sat on a low wall at the front and suddenly Gabriel leaned over and kissed me hard, before briskly walking home.. Needless to say that was a first; so a tick in the box for one's adolescent 'to do' list.

Chapter Nine

We prepare to take the war back into Europe

Now the time had come for the allies to undertake an assault on the mainland of Europe. It really seemed that the balance had tipped in our direction in Europe, although it was very hard going in Asia. German troops were still battling in Russia (At a meeting of the Soviet praesidium Joseph Stalin saidp, "It is in our interests to extend the war with Germany as long as possible to weaken them as much as we can.") The Allies were much strengthened by the arrival of American personnel and equipment.

At home there were significant developments for Reg and Grace. The YMCA premises were still crowded day and night with servicemen and women. There was accommodation for officers, but little for other ranks. Reg found some disused warehouses near to Piccadilly railway station, which the YMCA took over and turned into the King George Services Club with great airy dormitories with 100 single beds on each of four floors. There was a great modern kitchen, a lounge and a quiet room; the whole place staffed by volunteer workers. The YMCA opened an information bureau at the station. By now Grace had interviewed some 1,500 volunteer women and appointed 1,250.

I know that this place was still operating for some time after the war was over when there were still servicemen on the move, including Americans. in the summer of 1949 between school and university I did several evening shifts at the King George Club, either helping with food prep in the late afternoon or at the cash desk for the dormitories that opened at 7.p.m. By this time there were only two of the four floors of dormitories still in use. Doing food prep was together with Mrs Daish, who had been head cook, not chef, in a large London hotel and Fred, who had been a hotel porter. Both were retired, but came in on two or three afternoons a week to do their bit and to chat about old times..

An unexpected development was that The War Office appointed Reg as Army Welfare Officer for Manchester and outlying districts and Grace as Lady Army Welfare Officer for Manchester and suburbs. She didn't want it as she knew nothing about military procedures and practices and she was fully occupied with her YMCA duties. She was eventually persuaded, but refused to be paid anything but expenses and flatly refused to wear army uniform of Junior Commander ATS. She insisted on wearing her YMCA uniform. Reg never wore uniform but had a windscreen sticker saying "Army Welfare Officer".

Grace's second story

I had to wear a black armband, embroidered with a red W, for welfare. My duties were these:

1. Inspection of all sites where ATS or WRAF personnel were housed to ensure that ablutions were in order and to see that the girls had reading matter, soft furnishings and other

comforts.

2. To deal with cases of compassionate leave. These were numerous and entailed visiting many tragic homes, especially in the slums of the city.

3. To undertake the welfare of unmarried mothers during their pregnancy. In this I was greatly helped by the Church of England

4. To ensure that adequate hostel accommodation for girls within the City centre. There were virtually none when I took up my duties. I was encouraged by the co-operation of the YW.CA, The Catholic Women's League, The Salvation Army and, of course, by the YMCA, so that we had four good hostels.

At this time we had two cars, provided for my parents' duties, one was an estate car with partly wooden bodywork and one was an Austin saloon.

Margaret's story

I drove Mrs Torrington on her welfare duties, although she sometimes drove herself. I had originally been a volunteer in the YMCA canteen, but I volunteered for her welfare duties as I had learned to drive before I got married. It was interesting work and on one occasion we had to take an extremely pregnant young woman to hospital, where we arrived just in time! We quite often had flowers to deliver from military men serving abroad. Usually they were greeted with real joy, but once there were two separate bouquets for different women nearby to each other on the same estate. I took one and Mrs T. took the other. She was welcomed with enthusiasm; I was met with, "For God's sake take it away. I've got a new chap now and he'll be livid."

Gradually the sense of tension in the country eased. The

war was far from over, but the level of fear lessened and some more evacuees returned. The small number of Roedean girls who had been evacuated to Cockermouth in Cumbria all came back, and Manchester Grammar School, which had moved part of the School to Blackpool, had all returned. After School Certificate, Keith joined the History Sixth in 1942. I joined three years later in Upper 3c (modern). Keith went up to Peterhouse Cambridge to study History in 1944.

In London the tension was temporarily heightened as 1944 saw the introduction by the Germans of the doodlebug or flying bomb, an early guided missile powered by a motor cycle engine. It was of limited range and London was the only major city it could reach. It was a terrifying weapon as you could hear the buzz of its engine until the fuel ran out, followed by a short period of silence while people on the ground waited with bated breath until the silence was broken by the explosion, which either killed you or you breathed a sigh of relief. the use of the weapon gave added impetus to the invasion of France to demolish the launch site.

The country as a whole was well aware that it was no longer whether, but when we would invade, and where. It was an open secret that we would invade, but when was not yet definite and where was the subject of elaborate methods of deception. Potentially it could be anywhere between Dunkirk in the west to the beaches of Normandy to the east. Dunkirk had the advantage of being an established port, which could be used after the initial invasion to land equipment and supplies. it was also the shorter distance from England. Normandy had broad sandy beaches for easy landing of troops in the initial assault, but no large port.

The question of when the invasion would take place was a bone of contention between Churchill and Stalin, who had wanted it in 1941 to take German troops away from the Russian front. Churchill wanted it later because of the pressure he was feeling from the Pacific front, where the British colonies and dependencies were being overwhelmed by the Japanese.

Early in this period of waiting and preparation, there was another military event that has entered the history books – the Dambusters raid. officially named Operation Chastise, carried out by RAF 617 Flight of Wellington bombers commanded by 25-year-old Wing Commander Guy Gibson, whose mission was to breach a series of dams on rivers near the industrial centre of the Ruhr in Germany to seriously damage Hitler's military production. The essence of the scheme was for the bombers to fly in low along the River Ruhr, sending bombs to breach the dams, but the bombs were like no others. They were invented by a Yorkshire engineer, Dr Neville Barnes Wallis, who remembered skimming stones on the beach while on holiday as a boy; you first scour the beach for reasonably flat stones, then go as close as you can to the sea, bend over to the right to be as close as possible to the surface level of the water and flick the stone horizontally across the surface so that it bounces, carries on and on until gravity sinks it.

Barnes Wallis designed a bomb to replicate the action of the skimming stone but hitting the dam before it sank. The rehearsals with dummy bombs were carried out on the River Derwent in Derbyshire, close to where we now live. The navigational skill and risk to the aircrew of the operation are unimaginable. The dams were breached, the flow of water and resultant loss of life were considerable, but the effective damage to the German war machine was less than hoped for. Guy Gibson was a hero like Douglas Bader and was awarded VC, DSO, DFC before he died when he was piloting a Mosquito light bomber in 1944. The aircraft crashed over Holland, shortly after Gibson had been adopted as a Parliamentary candidate for Macclesfield in the forthcoming General Election.

British forces made an unsuccessful raid on the French port of Dieppe, which was easily repulsed, but there were two joint allied forays into Italy in July 1943. First there was an invasion of Sicily, which swept through the island rapidly although most of the enemy troops escaped to mainland Italy. Then the Fascist dictator Benito Mussolini was deposed in a coup, and a new government put out peace feelers to the allies, but the German troops stationed in Italy were under orders from Berlin to fight a determined rearguard action.

Having had an easy time in Sicily, the allies moved on to Italy, invading through the port of Salerno on 3rd September 1943.

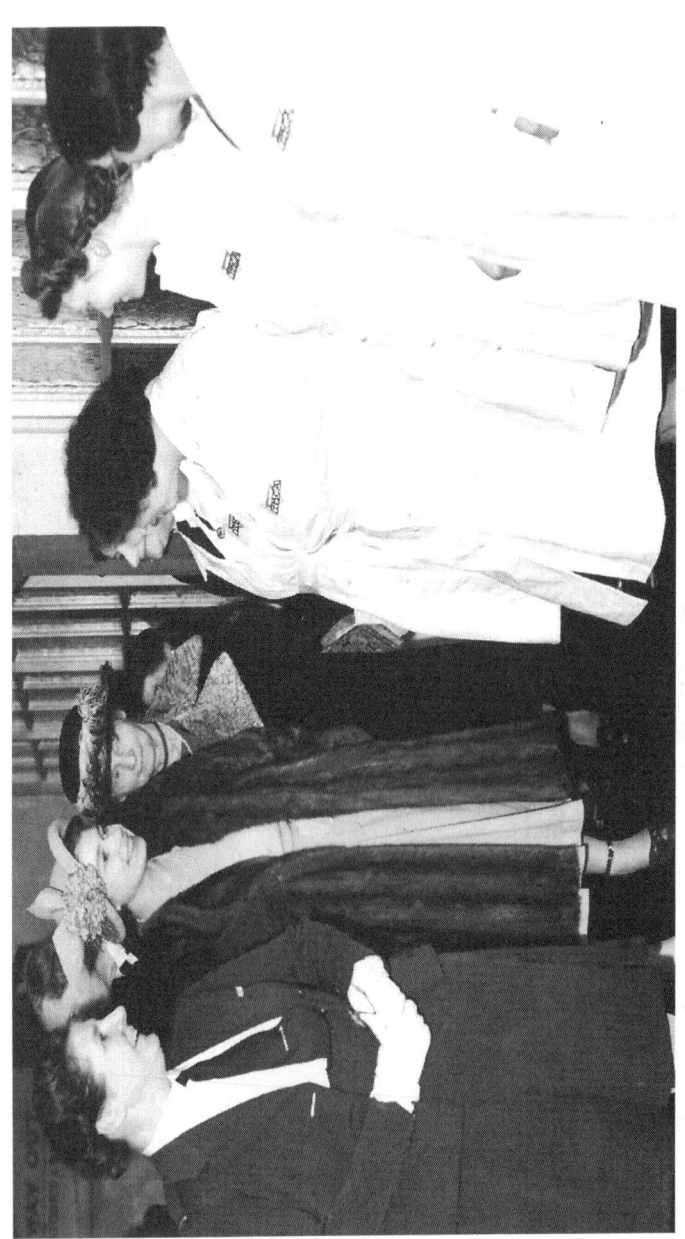

Grace introducing Princess Elizabeth to volunteers on a visit to the YMCA in Manchester

Signed photograph of Princess Elizabeth and
Prince Philip presented to Reg during their visit

Chapter Ten

D-Day and German Forces move back to defeat

D (for deliverance) Day was 6th June 1944, when Allied troops crossed the Channel and landed on German-occupied French soil to begin steadily fighting their way through France and then Germany towards Berlin. It was the largest seaborne assault in history, and the preparations took months, during which there was an elaborate campaign of disinformation by the British to conceal the intended landing point. The most devious of these was named, for some strange reason, Operation Mincemeat. They obtained the body of a tramp who had died after eating rat poison. They dressed him in the uniform of an officer in the Royal Marines and put papers in a pocket identifying him as Captain (acting major) William Martin.

Other papers revealed that the Allies were planning an attack on Sicily that was a feint to direct German attention away from Sardinia and Greece. where the real invasion was planned. This ensured a concentration of troops there while Normandy was sparsely covered until The Salerno landings demonstrated that Italy was being attacked seriously. Nothing was known of this extraordinary plot until after the war, when the man who devised it, Ewan Montague, described it in a book, and a film was made with the title "The Man Who Never Was".

Meanwhile Erwin Rommel was in overall command of the German troops preparing to repel the invasion, so he ensured that defences were widely spread along the French coast, but he personally believed the landings would be on the Pas de Calais.

The date of the landings depended on the weather and phases of the moon, and was eventually deferred from the 5th to the 6th of June 1944. Overnight there had been heavy bombardment of the coastal defences from the Royal Navy, and 24,000 airborne troops had landed behind them. At 6.30 a.m. the seaborne landing began, with landing craft taking ground troops to one of five stretches of coast line named Utah, Gold, Sword, Juno or Omaha. First to land were beach marshals to direct troops towards different destinations. The marshal on Sword beach was depicted in the film "The Longest Day" by Kenneth More a popular film star of the day who famously had his dog with him .It sounds like a typical British eccentricity, but maybe it was the film maker's fictional flourish.

The first task after landing was to get off the beach, no easy matter when facing skilled marksmen above or beyond you, who were absolutely determined to stop you and push you back into the sea. Those on Omaha beach had the hardest task as they had to scale a cliff.. Eventually all survivors of the relentless gunfire made it.

Once the beach heads had been secured, Mulberry harbours were brought into use. These were temporary ports designed and fabricated by British engineers in Plymouth that were towed across the Channel and to the beach heads to provide access for shipping to land tanks and heavy equipment to strengthen the capability of the advancing troops. Existing French ports had been sabotaged by the retreating Germans. It was some time before repairs could be completed so Mulberry harbours were in use for longer than their designers anticipated.

Slowly but steadily allied forces advanced through France, Italy and the Low countries towards the ultimate goal of Berlin. After a year of bitter fighting against determined resistance.

Notes

Forty years after D-Day, my wife Barbara and I visited Arromanches, where Utah, Gold, Sword, Juno and Omaha were situated. Wreckage of Mulberry harbours were still visible for tourists .to photograph. We also visited war cemeteries, British, American and German. The German cemetery was a sombre place. Tombstones were very small and close to the ground. Above them was a legend. I recall it well but not accurately from the German as "Somewhere, some time, someone will answer the question. Why?"

The film *The Man Who Never Was* was produced in 1956. *The Longest Day* was produced in 1962. Both films are available on DVD and Blu-ray.

Grace on night duty at Manchester Piccadilly Station, giving advice on accommodation

Chapter Eleven

Victory in Europe and huge celebrations

After a year of bitter fighting against determined resistance from the Germans, the allied troops entered a ruined Berlin, which was now occupied by British and Commonwealth forces, Americans, Free French and Russian. The bodies of Hitler and his mistress, Eva Braun, were found in the ruins of his underground bunker. The next day the bodies of Joseph Goebbels and his wife Magda were found together with their six children, who had been poisoned by Goebbels with cyanide before he and Magda committed suicide.

Over the next few months most of the remaining members of the Nazi senior hierarchy were rounded up and held for trial as war. criminals..Some others escaped and went into hiding in South America..Various people wanted for war crimes were discovered and tried over the next 30 years. largely due to the efforts of Israeli Nazi hunters .

There were enthusiastic celebrations throughout the United Kingdom. All the main cities had gatherings in the city centre, with Manchester celebrating in Albert Square and Piccadilly Gardens. Cinemas showed continuous newsreels of the celebrations outside Buckingham Palace, with the King and Queen with the two princesses, then with Churchill, who invariably received a rapturous welcome.

Gradually the excitement calmed and some horrors emerged. We heard about concentration camps, where millions of people had been executed by being herded together in gas chambers. These had been liberated by the allies as they advanced. One of the first was Belsen, where British troops found 60,000 people emaciated and starving or seriously ill, together with 13,000 corpses strewn randomly around the camp. As the pictures appeared in cinemas and newspapers, one person was especially alarming, the deputy commandant, Irma Grese, who had a full head of pure blonde hair. She was arrested and tried in a British military court, found guilty of mass murder and hanged. She was twenty two and remains the youngest woman ever hanged in a British jurisdiction.

We had been wildly celebrating VE Day, but VJ day was still twelve months away with further horrors

Chapter Twelve

*The post-war world and
ex servicemen become teachers*

Although overwhelmed by VE Day, a minor happening in the Autumn of 1945 was that I became a pupil at The Manchester Grammar School (MGS), being now 14, but the impact of WW2 continued. My form master was Mr Lund, who gave us new boys a bit of a pep talk about the importance of joining such an illustrious school, where we were expected to develop a sense of effortless <u>and acceptable</u> superiority. "Never forget acceptable. No arrogance, but responsibility". He then went on to laud the contemporary arrival at school of a number of ex-servicemen,teachers who would no doubt enliven our teaching. One such was a man, O.J.Key, known as Oscar Joe, who had been a fighter pilot. MGS can be approached from the front or the back. The front has a quite impressive front drive and, at that time, nobody at all drove along it. Oscar Joe did, driving an ageing, open-top Lagonda. Quite an entrance!

Grace and Reg. gradually ran down their roles with the Military, although continuing for some time with the YMCA. Keith was at Cambridge. He had been declared as unfit for military service because of a mastoid operation he had a few years earlier..Nowadays the condition(an infection of the middle ear) is treated by anti-biotics.

There were Nuremberg trials of the 24 leading Nazis before an international tribunal under international law . The reason for choosing Nuremberg was that it was the location of the great Nazi and military rallies in the thirties..The hearings were Chaired by a British high court judge. The defendants were all found guilty and condemned to death by hanging. On the morning the executions were to be carried out, Herman Goering was found dead in his cell having committed suicide by swallowing cyanide. I heard about it while having my hair cut and it was the topic of conversation in the barber's shop, mainly disgust that he had "cheated justice", which seemed an odd grumble.

So the Nazi high command was gone, but not all the Nazis; in Germany the occupying allies ran a de-nazification programme to ensure that any remaining Nazis were re-educated. outside Germany a Jewish Austrian holocaust survivor Simon Wiesental dedicated his life to finding more lower ranked Nazis to be brought to justice

The management of the German nation was divided into four sectors, British, French, Russian and American, with Berlin being similarly divided and adjoining their sector in the country. Initially this worked fairly well, but before long Russia's post war objectives became clear and the boundaries in Berlin were barricaded. This led to the blockading of Russian Berlin so that no goods or equipment were allowed in

from the west by road, rail or canal. The allied response was the Berlin airlift. Planes flew in a constant pattern from

British airfields to airfields in the three allied sectors carrying all manner of supplies, including coal and coal dust, which was left behind when the coal had been unloaded, and the plane turned round for its return for reloading. At its peak an aircraft landed every second. This was the first major confrontation of the Cold War.

Notes

When the hangings took place, for some reason the job was given to an American master sergeant and a corporal, who had problems. The drop between the trapdoor and the ground was not long enough and the size of the trap door was not big enough, so that victims did not fall far enough quickly enough to die of a broken neck, but writhed in agony being strangled by the noose. The chaplain attending the executions promptly stopped proceedings for the gallows to be re-modelled.

In about 1956 I was earning my living in a company that made miners' cap lamps. At one point, because I could speak German, I was despatched to try and sell some cap lamps in East (communist) Germany. My experiences illustrated the suspicions of the time. I first flew to the British sector of Berlin , where I rented a Volkswagen and drove towards the crossing into East Germany. Here there was a queue of ten or fifteen American lorries, waiting outside to get out of East Germany back into the British sector. I showed my passport and was waved through onto a pre-war Autobahn towards my destination of Zwickau.

After an hour I stopped to ask some farm workers if I was

on the right way. Their reaction on seeing a western car was to run away. I drove on and duly arrived in Zwickau, where the company's Berlin agent had booked me a room for the night. After arranging time for dinner I went out for a look round the town. It was a very hot day, so I went into a shop to buy a cold drink. The woman in the shop promptly ran into the back and sent out her husband to serve me, as I was obviously dangerous. Continuing my walk with my bottle of lemonade I passed a church that was boarded up with a rough poster showing a man wearing a bishop's mitre blessing a bunch of nuclear missiles, but then a quite different surprise; The local cinema was showing "The Lavender Hill Mob" one of the very popular Ealing comedies of the time.

Returning to the hotel, it was soon time for dinner so I presented myself at the restaurant, wondering what my reception would be. The head waiter greeted me with a broad smile, my first of the day, saying, 'Ah, Herr Torrington?' 'Ya'. It looked as if we would be pals. He asked me to wait one moment and immediately hustled away the people sitting near to the only table set for one. Can you imagine the reaction of people in a western hotel in the middle of their meals to being asked to change tables? This lot moved without a murmur, taking their plates and cutlery with them, so I sat in solitary splendour.

The following day I visited my potential buyers and set off on my return journey to Berlin, where I was waved down by a man in impressive uniform, who examined my passport. I think he was Russian, although he spoke pretty good German, realising that I could too, he took me into his office for a coffee, where he threw back the shutters "to cool the room". I could see the car being rigorously searched by two underlings as we drank our coffee, after which We shook hands and I went on my way. To my surprise I heard a month later from our Berlin agent that an order for cap lamps had been placed.

Chapter Thirteen

It's Not Over Yet

So far this story has been about growing up during a European war, and in that context I have nothing to say about the continuing war in the Pacific against the Japanese. I can merely summarise what is well covered in books by well-qualified other people.

As a nation that was still the head of the British Empire we had a big interest, as Hong Kong and the Malay states with Singapore had already been overrun, and India was vulnerable. Neither Australia nor New Zealand were safe. We had been fighting against the Japanese in Burma since 1942.

Conditions were generally awful, entirely in jungle and stifling heat, against an enemy that was brutal and relentless. One that caused excessive hardship for British troops was the Japanese use of British and Commonwealth prisoners of war in building of a prospective railway through to India. The British officers believed that they should build the best possible bridge, but were thwarted by the interference and incompetence of their Japanese captors. .In1957 this incident was made into a Hollywood film "The Bridge on the River Kwai" starring Alec

Guiness. It is still possible to visit what remains of the bridge near the town of Kanchanaburi and to visit the British war cemetery with its distinctive grave stones in white Portland stone.

The war was being waged by British and Indian troops together with Gurkahs from Nepal under two Generals William Slim and Orde Wingate. both born in India. Gurkahs remain a significant element of the British Army to-day. The American "Vinegar Joe" Stillwell who hated theBritish, commanded U.S. troops alongside many Chinese.

At home it all seemed far away, especially as the wartime coalition government had collapsed and a general election was held in July 1945, barely a month after the European war had finished. To the amazement of many, and the delight of others, Winston Churchill was ousted as prime minister and a Labour government under Clement Attlee took his place. It seemed extraordinary that such a towering figure throughout six years of war leading to a satisfactory outcome should be voted out only days after he had been cheered by huge crowds throughout the kingdom.

It seemed to be for two reasons. Earlier he had been condemned for his actions in situations where members of the working class had demonstrated against poor living conditions; secondly, the labour party manifesto set out an attractive programme of social innovation, based on a report to the wartime coalition government in 1942 by Sir William Beveridge, a highly regarded economist.. It became known as The Beveridge Report. A contributory reason may have been Churchill's avowed determination to keep the British Empire intact at a time when its transformation was imminent.

However, he had no role in the final ending of the war twelve months later, when it was expedited by the horror of Hiroshima. An American bomber named Enola Gay dropped two atomic bombs on Japan, The first on the city of Hiroshima on 6th June 1945, which killed 146,000 people, the second on the city of Nagasaki three days later, which killed 80,00. The aircraft was piloted by Paul Tibbett, who died at the age of 92 after suffering poor health for many years.

Note

Barbara and I went to Kanchanaburi as tourists some years ago and stayed in the same hotel as was used by the Japanese officers. Apart from the associations it was extremely comfortable with a delightful River Kwai trickling along gently at the bottom of the hotel gardens.

Chapter Fourteen

The aftermath

Starting back at the domestic level, Reg had one more big project. Having spent the war dealing with military personnel, he wanted to go back to his beginnings with the YMCA, and the aims of its founders. he wanted to provide accommodation for young men working in the city and needing accommodation, so the idea of Montgomery House was born. First he had to raise the money, so he was back to working his contacts and eventually the foundation stone was laid by Field Marshall Lord Montgomery.

It was fashioned from a block of marble from the rubble of the city of Caen, one of the early places to be liberated by the British. The stone laying was carried out by Montgomery, wearing all his medals, displayed on a uniform in khaki serge, as worn by ordinary Tommies. When the building was complete Reg and Grace acted as joint wardens for a time, but his health was failing and he resigned from the YMCA and they set off on a cruise. By the time they reached Casablanca he had a collapse and they had to return. On December 15th 1958 he died after an operation on his duodenal ulcer.

Grace lived on until 1975 and enjoyed a visit to a Buckingham Palace Garden party as wells as being Chairman of the Manchester Women's Luncheon Club.

A fter Cambridge Keith joined the Civil Service in the Ministry for Aircraft Production, where he met and married Doreen. Moving on, he joined I.C.I in Billingham. In December 1960 he was returning from a conference in London and was collected from the station by an I.C.I car, which skidded on black ice and he was killed instantly, almost exactly two years after Reg.I went through university and then did two years national service with the R.A.F.one year of which was in Germany. After three weeks the military occupation came to an end, so I can honestly claim to have been there at the very beginning of the war with Germany and at its end..

The lessons of World War 1 had been learned. There were no punitive reparations for Germany to pay. Instead the rebuilding of the German economy was facilitated in the West at least, and we saw the "Wirtschaftswunder" or economic miracle in Western Germany. East Germany developed as a Communist country and part of the Soviet Union. Russia was now our enemy.

Winston Churchill, out of office, was in much demand as a speaker, in 1946 he was invited to deliver a speech in Fulton Missouri. He included the sentence "From Stettin in the Baltic to Trieste in the Adriatic an iron curtain has descended on the continent". This remains one of his great speeches and features in most dictionaries of quotations. Despite his addiction to cigars and his prodigious appetite for champagne and brandy, he lived for another 20 years and died in 1965 at he the age of 91, soon followed by his devoted American wife Clementine or

Clemmie. At his state funeral, the Prime Minister of Australia, Robert Menzies, began his tribute by saying, " The greatest heart in England has ceased to beat".

In 1947 Grace, Reg, Keith and I had a summer holiday in France, driving in our new Austin car, registration number DMH266, for which the French had supplied plentiful petrol coupons as part of a plan to attract more British tourists, as we were only allowed to take £50 pounds out of our country. Petrol coupons created a useful black market in selling spare ones to the French. Reg demonstrated a dubious morality in giving me (as the only French speaker in the family) the job of selling them.

As a naive sixteen year old who was I to disobey one who was both my father and a pillar of the community?. Driving through villages there were continuous celebrations commemorating their liberation two years earlier, including lots of flags and banners saying "Vive le General Leclerc".. Puzzled, I asked someone in one village who had liberated their village, and he replied, "Les Anglais" There's gratitude for you!

There is one more chapter to come, but at this point I close this chapter with two different voices. First, a poem written in 1940 by Harry Jessop, a sixty-year- old weaver from Yorkshire, of limited education, who found a voice in poetry:

YOUR PART AND MINE

Our island is threatened
then each man to his post
prepare to met this evil thing
which hovers round our coast

Our island home, yes yours and mine
tis here our kindred dwell
take up the cry, They shall not pass
nor make our lives a hell

Our island home it shall be free
the dead on Dunkirk sands
have given all they had, to save
these green and pleasant lands.

this island home we love so well
with all its faults is free
and no Gestapo shall decide
what we shall do, or be.

The lads upon the ramparts stand
a human bulwark there
Now let us give a helping hand
give now and do not spare

We must keep faith with those who died
to keep our island free
with those who shield us in the air
and on the rolling sea.

My second voice is quite different.. Barbara and I attend our local United Reformed Church. On Remembrance Sunday 2019 the 10.30 morning service was tailored to fit around the national commemoration at the Cenotaph in London. The BBC coverage would be projected on a screen at the front .

After a hymn and introductory prayer, our Minister, the rev. Dr Kirsty Thorpe talked of the need for remembrance to be more than reflection and nostalgia. She recounted an incident on Remembrance Sunday when she was ten years old in her childhood home in Portsmouth. She knew that at school the two minutes silence was always observed, but she never thought much about it, so her father took her to Thorney Island in Chichester harbour, where there was a graveyard alongside the parish church of Saint Nicholas.

A section of the graveyard was devoted to war graves containing graves of both commonwealth and German flyers. Thorney Island is very flat, so pilots in the Battle of Britain and later tended to head to it if their aircraft was in danger of needing to crash land because of damage. The unique feature of these graves was that each headstone was for two people; on the left was the inscription, "In memory of those who gave their lives for their country". On the right was the same inscription in German:|n errinerung an die, die sich das Vaterland gepfort haben.

Kirsty's father had explained that Commonwealth and German being buried side by side was a demonstration of reconciliation from which peace must follow.

In my mind I immediately thought of the despair in the words at the German graves at Arromanches, described in chapter nine, compared with the magnaminity and hope at Thorney.

Field Marshal Lord Montgomery laying the foundation stone of Montgomery House

A lifetime's achievement fulfilled – Montgomery House, 1956-57 Session

Chapter Fifteen

How some things have changed

Finally, an eclectic mix of things on the home front that are very different now compared with 1939/1945.

Antibiotics for combatting bacterial infection were first developed by Professor Alexander Fleming Professor of Bacteriology at St Mary's Hospital, Paddington,, where he developed penicillin after an accidental discovery in a Petri dish in 1928. After more work by more bacteriologists a range of anti biotics came into practical use by doctors with the advent of the National Health Service in 1946.

Beards were worn by very few men.. More commonly by sailors and occasional celebrities like George Bernard Shaw, the dramatist. Now they appear on many fashion conscious men, usually as a version of the Van Dyke, avoided by most politicians.

Bedclothes Sheets, blankets and counterpanes were what one had as a covering in bed at night at home. duvets were unknown.

Bill Bryson the American turned Briton who toured around the country in the 1980s describes his bewilderment at checking in to a coastal town when first arriving to find various instructions in his room, including, "please remove the counterpane when retiring". Baffled after spending some time fiddling with the window he visited the local libray the following day to get a definition of the strange word "counterpane".

Books were popular, although supply had been limited during the war, they were read by increasing numbers of people. School textbooks were gradually up-dated, as they were mainly re-war. German text-books were odd as examples of life in Berlin on the Unter den Linden was a completely different from the bomb shattered reality we knew from the newsreels we were seeing daily. Years later while doing national service in Germany after the military occupation had ended, postage stamps all had a surcharge of one pfennig, "notopfer Berlin" towards the cost of rebuilding the capital city.

Now books are changing with the development of digital books that you can read in your hand. I have a personal interest in what is happening to University text books as I am the lead author of a book that has been constantly in print since 1989, and the 11th edition to be published early in 2020, and for the first time t will be in print and as an ebook

Capital punishment was still the standard method of punishing convicted murderers. .After the Jury had returned the verdict of guilty, the judge would place a black cap on his head and pronounce to the prisoner that he would be taken to a place of execution and there "hanged by the neck until you are dead". The last execution was in 1964; the penalty was suspended in 1965 for murderers but retained by traitors until 1969 completely. The last woman to be hanged , for murdering her husband, was Ruth Ellis in 1958; the last traitor was William Joyce in 1946. He was a British Nazi, living in Berlin who broadcast Nazi propaganda in English in an affected upper class accent, so that the British press labelled him "Lord Haw-Haw".

Central heating in private houses was very rare. Open coal fires or gas heaters were the norm. Now central heating by oil or gas-fired boilers piping hot water through radiators is standard in new properties, although new forms will soon be needed to reduce atmospheric pollution further.

Computer Although the first device resembling the modern device was built by Alan Turing in 1936, the stimulus that followed during World war 2 was by the de-coders in Bletchley Park in attempts to break coded messages used by the German military. The first personal computers were produced between 1975 - 1984, one of them was the ZX21, invented by Sir Clive Sinclair, a British inventor who had earlier developed the pocket calculator and, later, an electric car that was a flop because it was too small for practical use.

Greetings and namings Greeting someone was normally "Hello" or "How do you do?" and never an embrace or Hug, except with family members. Men and adolescent boys had first names known as Christian names, yet typically addressed each other using surnames…. We referred to our parents collectively as "my parents" or. separately as "My Mother or My father" .

Within the family it was usually "Mum or Dad". More recently it has become the practice to refer generally to parents as "Mum or Dad". How to address parents in law is a problem usually but not always by using first names.

Female dress Trousers were seldom worn, although hats were on show on formal occasions. I spent 30 years as a lay magistrate in the 1970s/80s, and this was a time of change. Within weeks of me starting women had stopped wearing hats on the bench and a few began wearing smart trousers. The practice of women wearing hats in church had largely died out.

Male clothing In 1945 most adult males wearing long trousers had the bottom 3 or 4 cms turned up, not by the owner but turned up and ironed in the production process. This fashion continued for many years. It did not affect uniforms..Shirts were buttoned up and worn with a tie, a style maintained in some work places and in some school uniforms. Hats (trilby or bowler) were worn out of doors. Men did not wear hats in church and this practice is widely maintained.

Newspapers were purchased or delivered (as was milk) to the home..The reading of a printed daily paper is slowly declining as they become available digitally.

Phones In both 1939 and 1945 phones were telephones in a specific place and consisting of a micro phone to speak into and an earpiece for hearing what the other person was saying. The instrument was in a moulded body connecting the two elements and in rested on a piece of equipment that did two things; first in connected the users to whoever they wished to speak and then it disconnected the conversation when required, the connection being by a landline to a network of users, whose numbers were listed in a directory.

One evening Keith and I were home alone and bored, so we looked through the telephone directory to find all the numbers of people with the name Smelley; there were three, so we dialled them one by one saying "Are you Smelley? They all said Yes", so we rang off quickly.

Television was invented by the Scot John Logie Baird, who suffered poor health, especially eyesight, so he re-located to Hastings, where most of his work was done. He produced a crude model in 1936 and gradually modified until a feasible system was possible. It was adopted by the BBC and came into use by the 1950s, when many people watched the coronation of Elizabeth the second in 1953, mostly by clustering round a neighbour's television set, as few people could afford their own. The picture was small and in black and white, with only one channel. Colour and channel choice came later. For much of the twentieth century we rented our television set because of their relatively high cost to purchase.

Washing one's hands and face in a basin remains unchanged, but then washing the rest of you was in a bath. Showers were rare but now are standard and en suite facilities are more and more popular. Washing clothes was typically done by hand in a basin or sink and then squeezed through a mangle to remove most of the water before being pegged out an a washing line in the garden to dry. washing machines developed gradually

through the century through twin tubs to the division of washing from drying, now in a different machine of its own. The process was improved by moving from "dolly blue" tablets to the more sophistica ted methods of roday
.

The worldwide web or internet was invented by Sir Tim Berners-Lee from Birmingham while he was working at Cern in Switzerland in 1989.It was not imaginable in 1945,yet now it is used throughout the world and has spawned social media in all its extraordinary and expanding variations.

The YMCA has changed and is now a worldwide body headquartered in Geneva. It claims to be the largest youth organisation in the world.

My last word

My overwhelming impression of these few years of my young life is of the many ways that people "did their bit". The main contribution obviously was from members of the armed forces, in many cases losing their lives, and not all of them were called up, but volunteered. in the final years of the war I was able to watch at Old Trafford cricket ground when there were matches between the Royal Australian Air Force and various local teams.

The star Australian was Keith Miller – one of the greatest all-rounders. He had volunteered to come to to help in the Battle of Britain and remained till the end. He was tall and had a real swagger; he was the only batsman I have ever seen who could drive on the off side to just short of the boundary and then <u>start</u> walking to the other end. I have never seen anyone else walk the full distance. A few years later a journalist asked him if he felt the stress of playing international. cricket. He replied, "Stress? If you've flown an aircraft with a Messerschmitt up your arse, that's stress. Cricket is a game I love, no stress is involved"

I think of Carolyn's Uncle Cecil waiting in only his underpants while waist deep in water; I think of Mary's father who was shipwrecked off West Africa, so that his family didn't see him for eighteen months, but I also think of the large numbers of women volunteers who worked eight hour shifts to keep the YMCA canteen open non-stop throughout the war, and others who made beds and cleaned dormitories.

You have read about Philip's grandfather Jack Peacock who wanted to do more than help manufacture miners' lamps to ensure supplies of coal so he became a volunteer fire fighter as well.

My other main thought is that I lived at a time of Winston Churchill having his finest hour. I heard his wartime speeches. The Oxford Dictionary of Quotations has 34 entries from these, but I <u>heard</u> them, and the delivery transformed them from being impressive to being electrifying and had a powerful effect on those who heard them live, and he undoubtedly was able to galvanise the nation, no matter what their political party affiliation.

Thank you for reading this book,

Derek

Printed in Great Britain
by Amazon